T0031693

CHILI TIME, Y'ALL

How Texas Found Its
State Cuisine

WRITTEN BY JENNIFER COLEMAN
ILLUSTRATED BY KAY MEADOWS

PELICAN PUBLISHING
NEW ORLEANS

ISBN: 9781455626922
Ebook ISBN: 9781455626939

Printed in Korea

Published by Pelican Publishing
New Orleans, LA
www.pelicanpub.com

To Jocelyn and Kristi—thanks for a lifetime of memories
—JC

For Josiah
—KM

Chili became the official state dish of Texas when Governor Dolph Briscoe signed House Concurrent Resolution No. 18 (HCR 18) on May 11, 1977.

Cool north winds blowing makes Texans hunger for comfort food. Nothing cuts the chill like a big Bowl of Red!

Chili is a meat stew cooked with chili peppers. Texas cowboys in the 1800s made it popular. Red chili peppers supercharged the cowboys after a long, hard day working to move cattle.

Chile = The chile pepper itself, while
Chili = the spicy meat stew.

Texas chili is made from cubed chunks of meat instead of ground beef. Real Texas chili has NO BEANS.

Chiles were easy to find on the dusty cattle drive trails. As the cowboys moved north from Texas into Oklahoma, sometimes the cooking pot would get thin. With less meat in the chili, beans would fill in.

A Bowl of Red is a bowl of tradition. Beloved chili recipes are passed down from one generation to the next.

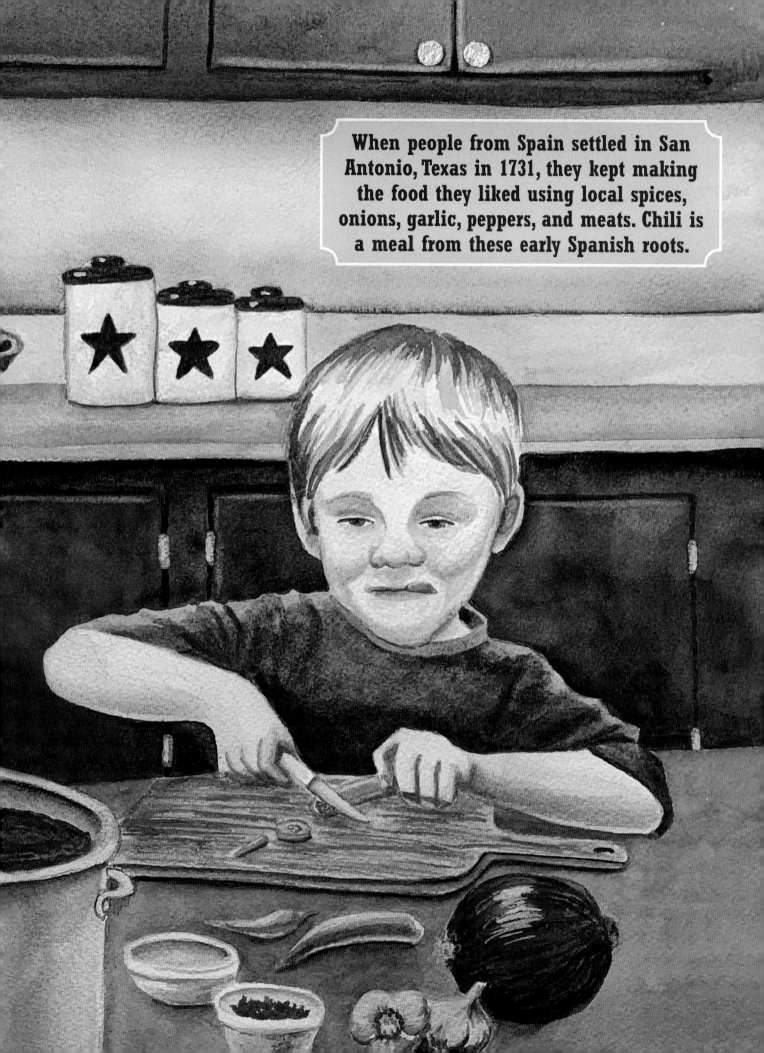

When people from Spain settled in San Antonio, Texas in 1731, they kept making the food they liked using local spices, onions, garlic, peppers, and meats. Chili is a meal from these early Spanish roots.

Today, people might use crock pots to cook chili over low heat for a long time.

Yet from 1860-1940, the San Antonio "Chili Queens" served their chili from pots over small open fires in the plaza at sunset.

Chili Queens were skilled mothers and daughters known for mouth-watering home cooking. The low flames they used could make even tough cuts of meat like antelope, goat, or venison soft and delicious. For only one dime, hungry diners filled a plate with chili and a tortilla and ate like a king.

Food this good should be shared far and wide. In 1881 a Texas Ranger was the first person to think to put chili in a can so that people outside of Texas could have a taste.

Texas Ranger and businessman William Tobin (1833-1884) picked up a love for chili when he was the city marshal for San Antonio. In 1881 he worked with the U.S. government to sell chili in a can to the army and navy.

In 1893 Texas chili gained fame when Texans set up a chili stand at the famous Chicago Expo. People came to the big fair to try new things and Texas chili stood out as a star.

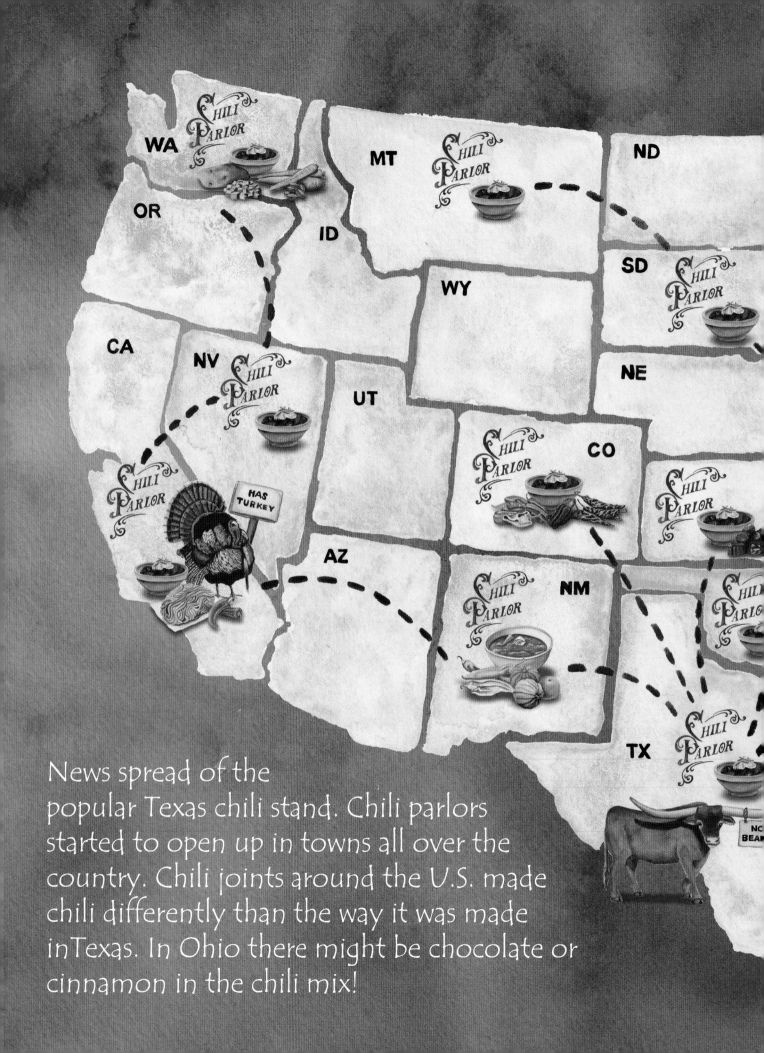

News spread of the popular Texas chili stand. Chili parlors started to open up in towns all over the country. Chili joints around the U.S. made chili differently than the way it was made in Texas. In Ohio there might be chocolate or cinnamon in the chili mix!

In 1895 a Texas ranch cook named Lyman T. Davis
made up his own chili recipe.

Lyman T. Davis

Mr. Davis brought his chili to a nearby oil boomtown. Out of the back of a horse-drawn carriage, a bowl of Davis's chili sold for five cents a bowl.

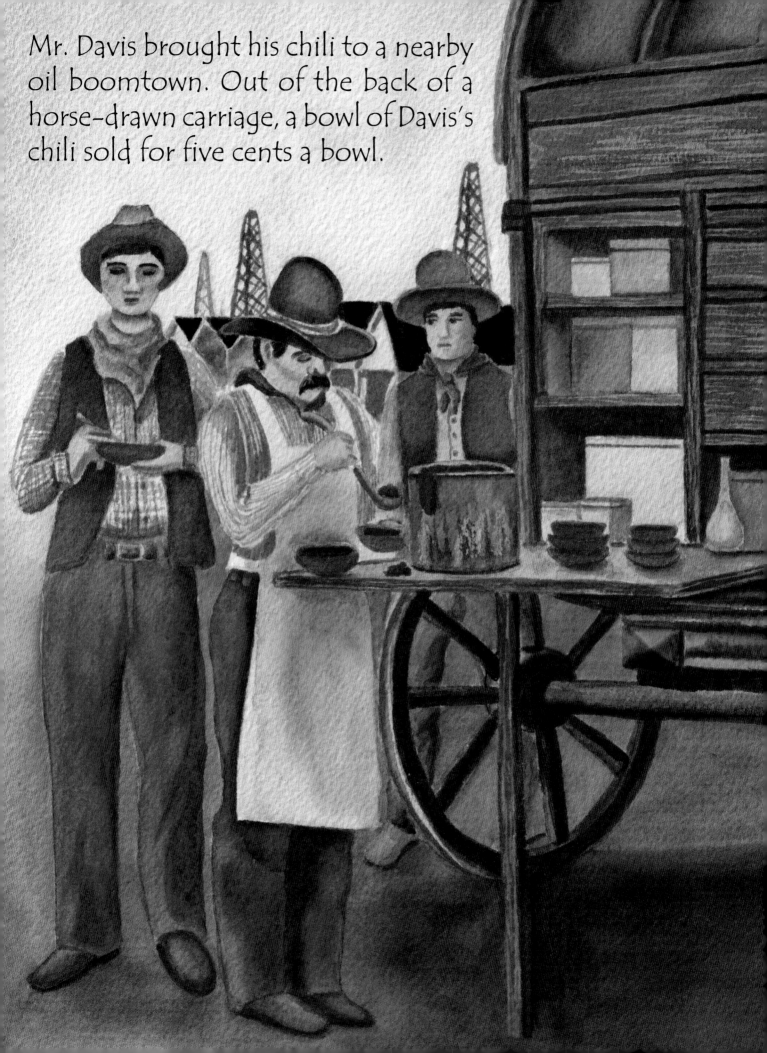

By the early 1920s, word of Davis's chili's greatness had gotten around. He began canning the chili. Mr. Davis's pet wolf, Kaiser Bill, was soon picked to be on the can's label.

That chili now had a name. **Wolf Brand** chili became famous and is still sold in stores today.

So how did chili become the official state dish of Texas?

Albert Agnor

Two men got together to ask the Texas government. One man with the idea was the world chili champion, Albert Agnor, and the other man was Texas lawmaker, Ben Z. Grant.

Ben Z. Grant

There was a **tough** battle of words on the House floor because barbeque fans wanted the official title.

Ben Grant argued that "chili had begun as a poor man's solution for preparing tough beef." Mr. Grant reminded people that "even President Lyndon Johnson had said anything outside of Texas pretending to be chili was just a poor substitute for the real thing."

On this day **May 11, 1977**
the State of Texas
hereby proclaims that the

Official State Food

shall be

CHILI

Dolph Briscoe
TEXAS GOVERNOR SIGNATURE

DOLPH BRISCOE
GOVERNOR OF TEXAS

Grant's argument for chili over barbecue won. Chili became the official state dish of Texas on May 11, 1977.

Texans enjoy their state dish in many ways. Chili might be spooned over a baked potato and dolloped with sour cream, cheese, or jalapenos. Some Texans pour chili right into a bag of corn chips at a football game.

No matter when, where, or how...
it's Chili Time, Y'all!

Stonewall, Texas

MRS. LYNDON B. JOHNSON'S RECIPE FOR...

PEDERNALES RIVER CHILI

4 POUNDS CHILI MEAT
    (COARSELY-GROUND ROUND STEAK OR WELL-TRIMMED CHUCK)

1 LARGE ONION, CHOPPED

2 CLOVES GARLIC

1 TEASPOON GROUND OREGANO

1 TEASPOON COMINO SEED

6 TEASPOONS CHILI POWDER (OR MORE, IF NEEDED)

1 1/2 CUPS CANNED WHOLE TOMATOES

2 - 6 GENEROUS DASHES LIQUID HOT SAUCE

2 CUPS HOT WATER

SALT TO TASTE

    PLACE MEAT, ONION AND GARLIC IN LARGE, HEAVY PAN OR DUTCH
OVEN. COOK UNTIL LIGHT IN COLOR. ADD OREGANO, COMINO SEED, CHILI
POWDER, TOMATOES, HOT PEPPER SAUCE, SALT AND HOT WATER. BRING
TO A BOIL, LOWER HEAT AND SIMMER FOR ABOUT 1 HOUR. SKIM OFF FAT
DURING COOKING.

★   U.S. President Lyndon B. Johnson was a BIG chili lover, especially of his wife's version. LBJ's favorite recipe became known as Pedernales River chili after the location of his Texas ranch.

Other Fun Facts!

★   The official signing ceremony naming chili the official state dish of Texas.

★ National Chili Day is the 4th Thursday in February.

★ Every year, The Chili Appreciation Society International supports over 400 sanctioned chili cook offs involving thousands of people.

★ Jesse James (1847–1882), outlaw of the old American West, refused to rob a bank in McKinney, Texas because that is where his favorite chili parlor was located.

HOUSE CONCURRENT RESOLUTION

WHEREAS, One cannot be a true son or daughter of this state without having his taste buds tingle at the thought of the treat that is real, honest-to-goodness, unadulterated Texas chili; and

WHEREAS, Texans continue today the tradition begun in San Antonio 140 years ago of making the best and only authentic concoction of this piquant delicacy; and

WHEREAS, President Lyndon B. Johnson commented that "chili concocted outside of Texas is a weak, apologetic imitation of the real thing," and Will Rogers described Texas chili as "the bowl of blessedness"; and

WHEREAS, Texas has been the site of the annual International Chili Cook-Off since 1967 and is the home of the 1976 World Champion Chili Cooker, Albert Agnor, of Marshall; and

WHEREAS, It is customary for the legislature to designate certain state emblems in recognition of this state's great heritage and rich resources; and

WHEREAS The beauty of Texas trees and flowers is represented by the pecan and bluebonnet and the mockingbird is emblematic of our abundant and varied wildlife, but the internationally esteemed cuisine of this great state had received no official recognition and has no official symbol; now, therefore, be it

RESOLVED by the House of Representatives of the State of Texas, the Senate concurring, that the 65th Legislature in recognition of the fact that the only real "bowl of red" is that prepared by Texans, hereby proclaims chili as the "State Dish of Texas."